Getting into Tennis

Ron Thomas and Joe Herran

MACMILLAN
LIBRARY

First published in 2005 by
MACMILLAN EDUCATION AUSTRALIA PTY LTD
627 Chapel Street, South Yarra 3141

Visit our website at www.macmillan.com.au

Associated companies and representatives throughout the world.

National Library of Australia
Cataloguing-in-Publication data

Thomas, Ron, 1947–.
  Tennis.

  Includes index.
  For middle primary school students.
  ISBN 0 7329 9711 9.

  1. Tennis – Juvenile literature. I. Herran, Joe. II.
  Title. (Series: Thomas, Ron, 1947– Getting into).

796.342

Edited by Helena Newton
Text and cover design by Cristina Neri, Canary Graphic Design
Illustrations by Nives Porcellato and Andy Craig
Photo research by Legend Images

Printed in China

Acknowledgements
The authors wish to acknowledge and thank Sam and Ray Leetham for their assistance and
advice in the writing of this book.

The authors and the publisher are grateful to the following for permission to reproduce
copyright material:

Cover photographs: Tennis ball courtesy of Photodisc, and player courtesy of Photodisc.

Australian Picture Library, pp. 5, 7; Australian Picture Library/Empics, p. 23; Clive Brunskill/
Getty Images, p. 22; Alex Livesey/Getty Images, p. 25; Photodisc, pp. 1, 6; Picture Media/
REUTERS/Jamil Bittar, p. 30 (bottom); Picture Media/REUTERS/David Gray, p. 27; Picture
Media/REUTERS/Kim Kyung-Hoon, p. 30 (top); Picture Media/REUTERS/Jeff J Mitchell,
p. 9; Picture Media/REUTERS/Sergio Perez, p. 29; Picture Media/REUTERS/Mike Segar, p. 26;
Picture Media/REUTERS/Tim Wimborne, pp. 4, 28.

While every care has been taken to trace and acknowledge copyright, the publisher tenders
their apologies for any accidental infringement where copyright has proved untraceable.
Where the attempt has been unsuccessful, the publisher welcomes information that would
redress the situation.

Contents

Glossary words

When a word is printed in **bold**, you can look up its meaning in the Glossary on page 31.

The game

Tennis is a popular sport with both young and older people who play in local, district and state competitions. The game is played outdoors and indoors.

Tennis is played in countries all over the world. International tennis is governed by the International Tennis Federation (ITF), which was formed in 1913 as the International Lawn Tennis Federation. The ITF sets the rules for tennis and monitors international competitions. The ITF has 201 national tennis association members.

Martina Navratilova of the United States of America and her mixed doubles partner Leander Paes of India at the Australian Open Tennis championship in Melbourne in 2004

The history of tennis

A game similar to tennis called *le jeu de la paume*, meaning 'the game of the hand', was played by monks in monasteries in France during the 1000s. It was also known as *tenez*, meaning 'hold this.' Players hit a cloth bag stuffed with hair, back and forth over a cord with their open hands. In England, from about 1500, a game known as Real or Royal Tennis was played using a wooden-handled racquet strung with sheep gut. The first game of tennis on a grass court was played in Birmingham, England, in 1858. From this time the modern game developed and spread to countries around the world.

Did you know?
The first tennis championships at Wimbledon were held in 1877.

4

Playing a match

Tennis players aim to hit a ball over a net and into an area of the court in such a way that opposing players cannot return it. There are two opposing players in a singles match and four players, two pairs, in **doubles** matches. Players aim to win more games than their opponents.

To begin a singles match, one player, known as the **server**, stands behind the **baseline** and hits the ball across the net to the opponent's side. The opponent is known as the **receiver**. Players then hit the ball back and forth until one player hits the ball into the net, hits it outside their opponent's court, or until one player hits a shot that their opponent cannot return.

Scoring starts at zero, called **love**, and then points increase to 15 for the first, 30 for second and 40 for the third point. The next point, called game, wins the game. When a player has won six games and is ahead by two games, they have won the **set**. In most tournaments for men and women, the first player to win two out of three sets wins the match. But in men's Davis Cup and Grand Slam tournaments, three out of five sets must be won to win the match.

An umpire, assisted by linespersons, controls play.

Tennis players stand on either side of the net while an umpire and linespersons watch from the sides.

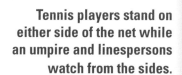

Rules
The choice of ends of the court and the right to be server or receiver in the first game is decided by a coin or racquet toss.

Equipment

The equipment used in tennis competitions must all meet the standards set by the sport's governing body.

The racquet

The racquet has a long, straight handle and an oval frame. Younger players use shorter racquets and the length increases as the player grows. According to the rules, a tennis racquet should be no longer than 73.66 centimetres (29 inches) and no wider than 31.75 centimetres (12.5 inches).

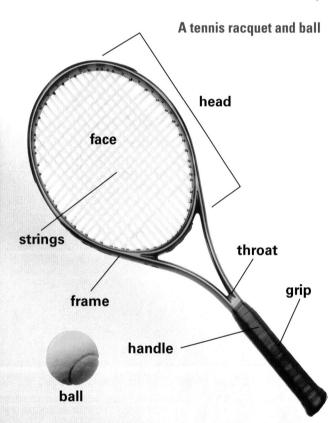

A tennis racquet and ball

head

face

strings

throat

grip

frame

handle

ball

Racquet frames are made of metals such as steel, titanium or aluminium, or a combination of metals as well as plastics or fibreglass. The racquet head consists of the frame and the strings. Racquet strings form a criss-cross pattern and are made of artificial or human-made materials, or from natural gut, which comes from sheep or pig intestines. The strings are the playing surface or 'face' of the racquet. The **grip** size needs to be large enough for a player's thumb and forefinger to touch around it. The throat is the thin area of the racquet handle where it meets the head.

Tennis balls

Tennis balls are round, hollow balls made of rubber, filled with pressurised air and covered with yellow or white wool and nylon fabric. They measure between 6.23 and 6.67 centimetres (2.5 to 2.6 inches) across.

Clothing

Some clubs enforce a rule that says that tennis players must wear white clothing, but a wide range of colours is worn at other clubs. Tennis clothing needs to be comfortable and loose enough to allow plenty of room for movement. Men wear shorts and short-sleeved shirts. Women wear dresses, or a short-sleeved shirt with a skirt or shorts.

Tennis shoes and socks

Shoes cushion the player's feet and have flat soles with enough grip to prevent slipping. Shoes need to fit well and be comfortable. Socks made of cotton absorb sweat and keep the player's feet comfortable.

Sweatbands and sun protection

Sweatbands are worn on the head and wrists to help soak up perspiration. To protect their skin from the harmful rays of the sun, players use sunscreen. Wearing a cap or visor on hot days is a good idea too.

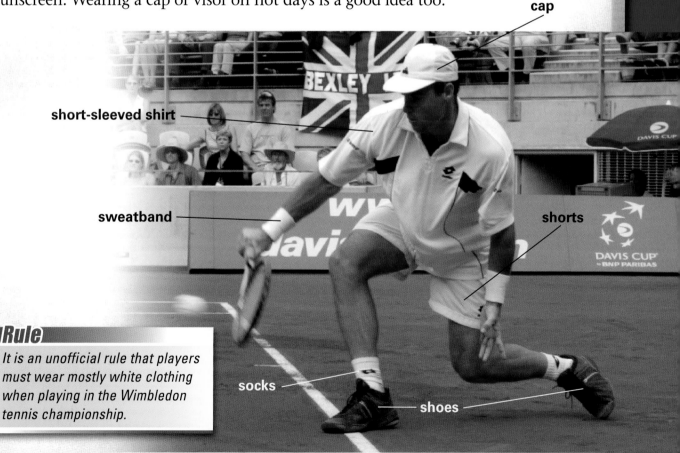

cap

short-sleeved shirt

sweatband

shorts

socks

shoes

Rule

It is an unofficial rule that players must wear mostly white clothing when playing in the Wimbledon tennis championship.

The court

Tennis is played on a rectangular court of grass, clay or an artificial material.

A tennis court

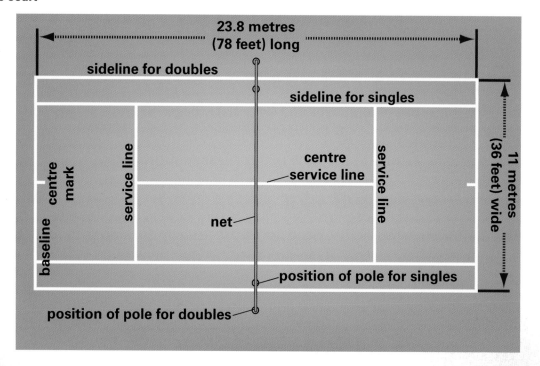

The net

The net, supported by two poles, runs across the centre of the court and is 91.4 centimetres (36 inches) high in the centre. The strip of white canvas at the top of the net is the band.

A tennis net

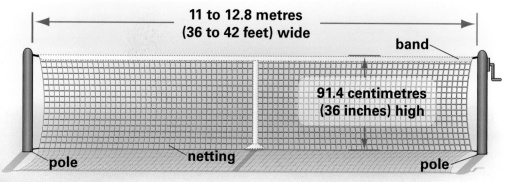

The players

The players stand on opposite sides of the net. In singles matches the player who first hits the ball is known as the server. The other player is the receiver. The choice of ends and the right to be server or receiver is decided by a coin or racquet toss. The player who wins the toss can:

The players aim to hit the ball over the net in a way that makes it difficult for the opponent to return the ball.

- choose to serve
- choose to receive
- choose ends
- ask the opponent to choose.

At the end of the first game, the receiver becomes the server. Players continue to change roles for all games that follow.

Changing ends

Players change ends:

- at the end of the first, third, fifth and then every alternate game of each set
- at the end of each set if the total number of games is uneven
- at the end of the first game of the next set if the total number of games in the previous set was even.

Did you know?

The modern game of tennis was invented by Major Walter Clopton Wingfield in 1873.

Skills

Beginning players learn the basic skills of tennis, such as holding and handling the racquet, taking the correct stance, serving and receiving service using a variety of shots. With practice, players develop these skills and improve their performance.

The eastern forehand grip

The western forehand grip

The continental grip is often called the chopper because it is the grip used to grip an axe while chopping wood.

The grip

There is a number of ways that a player holds or grips the racquet. The player changes grips depending on the shot being played.

Forehand grips

The eastern forehand grip is sometimes called the 'shake hands' grip because the palm is placed behind the handle and the thumb is wrapped round the handle as though the player is 'shaking hands' with the racquet. This is the most common grip in tennis and is used for the **forehand** drive, **volley** and **lob**. In the western forehand grip, the player's palm is underneath the handle. This grip is used to hit balls at about waist height.

The chopper or continental grip is halfway between the eastern forehand and the **backhand** grip, and is used for serves and for the volley. The player's palm is on top of the handle and the thumb is wrapped around the handle.

Backhand grips

There are two ways of holding the racquet for backhand strokes, the eastern backhand grip and the two-handed or double-handed backhand. For the eastern backhand, the palm of the player's hand is on top of the handle and the knuckles face upwards. The thumb is placed diagonally across the back of the handle. This grip is used for the backhand drive and the lob.

In the two-handed or double-handed backhand, the hand closest to the end of the racquet holds with a continental grip. The other hand is in an eastern forehand grip. Both hands touch on the handle. Using two hands gives the player greater power and better control when playing a backhand shot.

The eastern backhand grip

The double-handed backhand grip

The ready position

The ready position

Once the player has learned how to grip the racquet he or she is ready to play. When waiting to receive service, the player stands in the ready position. The body is relaxed, the legs are shoulder width apart and the knees are bent. The player's weight is on the balls of the feet ready to push off the ground. The player is also ready to move in either direction to get to the ball. The racquet is held out in front and centred, supported by the player's free hand.

The serve

The serve puts the ball into play. The server must not serve until the receiver is ready. The serving player aims to hit the ball over the net and into the service square diagonally opposite. If the ball hits the net but lands in, it is called a **let** and the ball is served again. To serve the ball the player follows these steps.

Rule

In singles matches, the players alternate service. In doubles, service alternates between the sides, and all four players serve in turn.

The serve

1 The player is sideways to the court and both feet are behind the baseline. The continental or chopper grip is used. The ball rests against the racquet.

2 The player tosses the ball into the air, slightly in front of the body. The ball is released when the arm is fully stretched.

3 The racquet is taken backwards as the ball rises. The knees are bent and the back is arched.

4 The player begins to jump up to swing the racquet head at the ball.

5 The legs are straightened and the ball is hit. The arm holding the racquet is fully stretched and the free arm is used for balance.

6 The player follows through, bending at the waist and letting the racquet pass around the waist.

Service faults

The server's feet must not touch the baseline or the inside of the court until after the ball has been hit. If this happens it is called a **foot fault**. The server is given two chances to make a good serve. The first mistake is called a **fault**. If the server receives a double fault, the receiver is awarded a point.

It is a fault if the serve fails to land in the receiver's service court; if the server swings and misses the ball entirely; or if the serve is made from beyond the baseline or from the wrong side of the centre mark.

Return of service

The receiver stands in the ready position when the serve begins. The ball is only allowed to bounce once before it is hit back over the net, so the receiver must move into a position where he or she is able to return the ball and keep it in play.

If the serve is slow, the receiver moves forward. If it is fast the player moves back and tries to block the return. By watching the ball carefully, the receiver can find clues as to where the server is going to serve. The player moves quickly into position, swings the racquet back and turns the shoulders and hips side-on to the ball.

▮Rules▮

The receiver who does not wait for a served ball to bounce before hitting it loses one point.

The receiver may stand in any position on his or her own side of the net while waiting for the serve.

Ground strokes

Ground strokes are played after the ball bounces. There are two types of ground strokes, the forehand drive and the backhand drive.

Forehand drive

The forehand drive is one of the basic shots in tennis and is usually the strongest stroke. The easiest grip to use for this shot is the eastern 'shake hands' grip. When the racquet is swung back, the player's palm is facing forwards. The player follows these steps to perform the forehand drive.

The forehand drive

1 The player stands in the ready position and focuses on the opponent and the ball.

2 The player's shoulders are turned side-on to the net and the racquet is taken back as soon as the ball leaves the opponent's racquet.

3 The player steps forward and takes the racquet back.

4 The racquet is swung through and up to meet the ball.

5 The player continues to move the racquet around to the front of the body.

6 To follow through, the racquet is brought up and over the shoulder. After the shot, the player assumes the ready position.

Backhand drive

When performing the backhand drive, the right-handed player makes a shot from the left side of the body, and the left-handed player makes a shot from the right side of the body, so that the back of the hand is facing forwards when the racquet is swung back. The eastern backhand grip is used for the backhand drive. The player follows these steps to perform the backhand drive.

The backhand drive

1 The player stands in the ready position. The eyes are focussed on the opponent and the ball.

2 The racquet is taken back and supported by the other hand, which turns the racquet to the eastern backhand grip.

3 The player, with knees bent, steps forward and swings the racquet through.

4 The racquet meets the ball in front of the body and hits it in an upward motion.

5 The player follows through, with the racquet following the direction of the ball.

6 The player completes the follow-through, raising the racquet higher. After the shot has been played, the player assumes the ready position.

The double-handed backhand drive

The double-handed backhand drive is played in the same way as a one-handed backhand shot but the player holds the racquet with both hands. This gives the player greater control of the racquet and means that the ball can be hit with more power.

The volley

A volley is a shot played before the ball bounces. It can be played forehand or backhand.

The forehand volley

The forehand volley is played close to the net to return the ball quickly. The player follows these steps to perform the forehand volley.

The forehand volley

1 The player begins in an attacking position about 2 metres (6.6 feet) away from the net. The racquet is held in a chopper or continental grip and supported by the free hand.

2 The knees are bent and the racquet is taken back no further than the shoulder and to a height slightly above the height at which the ball will be struck.

3 The player leans forward and hits the ball in front and to the side of the body. The free arm is used for balance.

4 The player follows through, keeping the knees bent.

The backhand volley

The action for the backhand volley is similar to that used for the forehand volley, but the supporting hand stays on the racquet until the ball is hit. The backhand volley can be used for a ball at or above net height. The player follows these steps for the backhand volley.

The backhand volley

1 The player begins in the ready position, holding the racquet in one hand in the continental grip and supporting it with the other.

2 Next, the player takes the racquet back slightly, still supporting the racquet with the other hand.
The player is side-on to the net.

3 The player steps forward to strike the ball with a strong push of the racquet, hitting it just over the top of the net.

The smash

The smash is the most powerful shot in tennis. It can be played after the ball bounces but is usually hit before the bounce, or on the full. The player uses the chopper or continental grip and aims to place the ball deep in the opponent's court and on the opponent's weaker side. The player follows these steps to perform the smash.

The smash

1 The player begins in the ready position.

2 The player moves under the falling ball, turning sideways to the net and pointing at the ball. The racquet is lifted high behind the head.

3 The player takes the racquet behind the shoulders, keeping the elbow high.

4 Next the player 'throws' the racquet head upwards and hits the ball at maximum stretch, slightly in front of the body.

5 The player follows through with the racquet, down and across the body.

Experienced players can jump to reach the ball when playing a smash.

The lob

The lob is a shot that passes high above the opponent's head and aims to force the opponent back from the net. The lob can be played forehand or backhand.

Forehand lob

For the forehand lob, the player uses the eastern forehand or continental grip to hit underneath the ball. The player follows these steps for the forehand lob.

The forehand lob

1 The player begins in the ready position.

2 The player is side-on to the net and takes the racquet back.

3 The player steps forward, swinging the racquet back as the ball starts to fall.

4 The racquet follows a steep upward path. The head of the racquet faces upwards to get the ball up into the air.

5 The racquet rises smoothly and hits the ball over the opponent's head. The knees are bent and the head is still.

6 The stroke finishes with a high follow-through. After making the shot the player returns quickly to the ready position.

Backhand lob

The backhand lob is used to hit the ball from the backhand side.

The backhand lob

The drop shot

The drop shot drops just over the net. It is an effective shot against an opponent who is playing at the baseline.

Forehand drop shot

The forehand drop shot can be disguised to look like a regular ground stroke, and can look as if the player intends to hit a drive. This shot can be used to confuse the opponent. The player follows these steps to perform the forehand drop shot.

The forehand drop shot

The racquet is taken back and held, using a continental grip, at shoulder height.

With knees bent, the player brings the racquet forward and under the ball. The racquet hits the ball in front of the body.

The follow-through lifts the ball gently over the net.

Rule

If the ball hits the net during play and then goes over the net it is considered a good ball and must be played.

Backhand drop shot

The backhand drop shot

The backhand drop shot can also be disguised to look like a drive shot, but the player slows the racquet down before hitting the ball.

Spin

Players put spin on the ball to change the angle, height, speed and flight path of the ball before and after the bounce. Spin is used to vary shots and confuse an opponent. There are two common types of spin, topspin and sidespin.

Topspin

Topspin is hitting the ball so that it flicks up and goes high. The player starts the shot with the racquet head near the ground and strikes the ball at about knee height with a sharp upward swing. The player's body swings round on the follow-through.

Putting topspin on the ball means that it spins and travels in a straight line.

Sidespin

Sidespin is also called 'slice' or 'backspin'. The player takes the racquet back high, well above the level of the oncoming ball. The racquet is swung across the direction of the ball. The side of the ball spins in the direction of travel, swerving in flight. Sidespin is also used during service.

Putting sidespin on a ball means that it swerves as it spins.

Rules

Tennis rules for all international competitions are formulated by the governing body for tennis, the International Tennis Federation (ITF). Players need to learn and understand the basic rules before they are ready to play tennis.

Point penalty

A point penalty costs a player one point in the current game. A point is lost:

- if the player fails to return the ball over the net before it hits the ground twice

The rules of tennis are enforced by the umpire.

- if the player volleys the ball before it has crossed the net

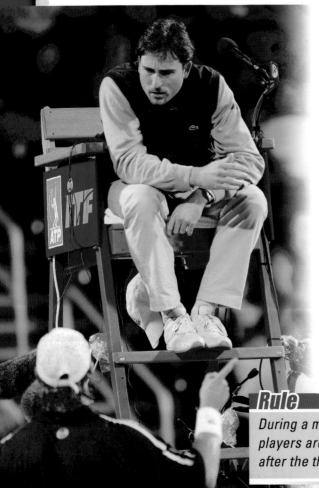

- if a returned ball hits the ground outside the opponent's court
- if the ball touches any part of the player's body other than the hands
- if the player touches the ball more than once with the racquet
- if the player catches or carries the ball on the racquet
- if the player changes the shape of the racquet during play
- for unsporting conduct such as swearing at an official, or delaying a game by arguing
- for throwing the racquet or hitting the ball in anger.

Rule

During a match, play is continuous, but in certain circumstances players are allowed to take a 10-minute break. Breaks can be taken after the third set for men and after the second set for women.

Scoring

Both players begin at love or zero points. The first point scored is 15, the second point is 30 and the third is 40. The next point, called game, wins the game. The server's score is given first. So, if the server scores first, the score is '15 love'. When both players have two points each the score is '30 all'.

When players are tied at '40 all', the score is '**deuce**'. At deuce, one player must win two points in a row to win the game. If the server wins the first point after deuce, the score is '**advantage** server'. If the server wins the next point they win the game. But, if the receiver wins the second point the score goes back to deuce. The game continues until one player wins 'advantage' and then wins the next point.

The first player to win six games wins a set. But, if the score reaches '5 games all', play continues until one player wins two games more than the opponent. This is called 'playing advantage'. When a game reaches '6 all', a tie-break is played. The original server serves first, then the other player serves twice. The game continues until one player has 7 points and is ahead by 2, or until one player is ahead by 2 after 7 points. Players change ends each time 6 points are scored.

PREVIOUS SETS

Officials

The officials at a tennis tournament include the referee, umpire, and linespersons or judges. **Ball boys and girls** also perform important roles at tennis tournaments.

Referee

The referee is the official who is in charge of a tournament. The referee does not officiate at matches, but may be asked by the umpire to interpret a rule. When this happens, the referee's decision is final.

Umpire

The umpire is the official who is in charge of a tennis match. The umpire sits in a raised chair at one end of the net. The umpire:

- calls the score after each point
- may reverse the decision of a judge or linesperson if it is clearly in error
- makes a decision if a judge or linesperson is unable to make it
- may impose point penalties or default a player for unsporting conduct.

The officials are positioned at various points around the tennis court.

1. linespersons or judges
2. baseline judges
3. service line judges
4. centre service line judges
5. ball boys or girls
6. chair umpire

Linespersons or judges

Linespersons or judges watch the lines on the court and state whether or not a shot has landed in the court. They signal their decisions to the umpire and players by calling 'out' or 'fault'.

Baseline judges stand in line with the baseline and are responsible for saying whether shots are in or out. Service line judges are responsible for saying whether a serve hits the court beyond the service line. Centre service line judges watch that the served ball lands in the service square diagonally opposite the server. All other judges rule whether balls are in or out and watch for foot faults.

Ball boys and ball girls

Ball boys and ball girls clear the court of tennis balls that have been hit out of play. They also pass tennis balls to the players as they are needed.

Ball boys and ball girls wait near the umpire's chair to clear away tennis balls during a match.

Player fitness

Tennis players need to be fit if they are to perform to the best of their ability. Running, swimming and cycling build stamina and fitness.

Warming up and stretching

Before a game or a practice session, it is important for tennis players to warm up all their muscles. This helps to prevent injuries such as muscle tears, strains and joint injuries. Gentle jogging helps players to warm up. Stretching makes players more flexible and helps the muscles and joints to move easily on the court.

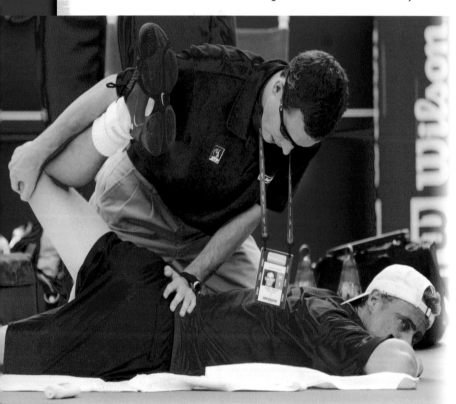

Sometimes the trainer helps the player to stretch to prevent injuries.

Neck stretches

The player tilts the head forward and slowly rolls the head to one shoulder and then the other. These exercises help to prevent stiffness in the neck and keep the neck flexible.

Shoulder stretch

The player stands upright and tries to try to touch the bottom of the shoulder blade with one hand, with the elbow pointing upwards. The other arm pulls back on the elbow of the bent arm. The player repeats the stretch using the other arm.

Side stretches

The player raises the right hand above the head and slowly leans to the left. The stretch is then repeated, leaning to the right. This stretches the waist and stomach muscles.

Calf stretches

The player places one foot in front of the other and leans forward, but keeps the back heel on the ground. The player pushes forward until the calf muscle in the back leg stretches. The stretch is repeated for the other leg.

Thigh stretches

Standing on one leg, the player holds the ankle of the raised leg. The player pulls the foot back to stretch the thigh, keeping the knees close together. The player can lean against a wall or hold onto another player for balance. The stretch is then repeated for the other leg.

Back stretch

The player crouches down on all fours with the head up and back flat. Then the player tucks the head under and arches the back upwards. The player feels the stretch in the upper back.

Groin stretch

The player sits on the ground with the knees bent and pointing out to either side. Holding onto the ankles, the player pulls them gently in towards the body. The player pushes down gently on the thighs with the arms so that the legs move towards the ground.

Hamstring stretch

Standing with one leg straight and the other slightly bent, the player places the hand on the thigh of the straight leg and bends forward slowly. The stretch is then repeated, keeping the other leg straight and placing the hand on the other thigh.

Stretching exercises, such as a standing hamstring stretch, are done in an easy and relaxed way and each position is held for at least 10 seconds.

The International Tennis Federation (ITF) is the governing body for tennis. It is a federation of national tennis associations from countries around the world. The role of ITF is to:

- set rules and specifications for equipment and facilities, and other regulations for all international and Olympic competitions, and wheelchair tennis
- appoint all international referees
- regulate the transfer of players between countries
- control all international competitions
- enforce an anti-doping program.

Nenad Zimonjic of Serbia and Montenegro playing a smash beside his mixed doubles partner, Elena Bovina of Russia, during the Australian Open in Melbourne, 2004

The Grand Slam

There are four yearly tournaments in the International Open Championships or the tennis 'Grand Slam'. They are the Australian Open played in Melbourne, the French Open played in Paris, the US Open played in New York and England's Wimbledon championship. The competitions at these tournaments are the men's and women's singles, and men's, women's and mixed doubles. There is also a junior singles and doubles competition for boys and girls from 13 to 17 years old.

Davis Cup

The Davis Cup is a men's tennis competition. Teams representing more than 100 countries take part each year. Players compete in singles and doubles matches. American Dwight Filley Davis first offered the Davis Cup as a prize in 1900.

The ITF Women's Circuit

The ITF Women's Circuit offers 300 tournaments in 61 countries. Winners and finalists qualify to join the Women's Tennis Association (WTA) World Tour.

The Federation (Fed) Cup

The Fed Cup is the top team competition in women's tennis. The competition began in 1963 to celebrate 50 years of the ITF. It continues each year with teams representing almost 100 countries.

Women's Tennis Association (WTA)

The WTA was formed in the 1970s by a group of professional women tennis players led by American star player, Billie Jean King. They felt that the prize money being offered to women was unfair compared to the prizes for professional male players. The first WTA event was held in the United States of America in 1970. In 2004, more than 1000 professional women tennis players, representing 76 nations, took part in the WTA World Tour in 31 countries. Millions of people attended these events and millions more watched on television.

The Belgian team celebrating their Fed Cup win in 2001

Seeding

Before a tournament, professional players are ranked or 'seeded' based on their ability and recent performances. The top-ranked player is called the top seed. Matches are arranged so that the top-seeded players will not meet until the later rounds of the tournament.

Olympic tennis

Britain's Tim Henman during a match at the 2004 Athens Olympic Games

Tennis was an Olympic event from 1896 until 1924, when it was discontinued. In 1896, it was an event for men only. At the Olympic Games in Paris in 1900, tennis became one of the first Olympic sports in which women were allowed to compete. Tennis was reintroduced as an Olympic sport at the Seoul Games in 1988.

There are four Olympic tennis events, men's singles, women's singles, men's doubles and women's doubles. The International Olympic Committee (IOC) recognises the ITF as the tennis authority.

Wheelchair tennis

The International Wheelchair Tennis Federation (IWTF) organises events for tennis players who use specially designed wheelchairs. The events follow ITF rules, except that the ball is allowed to bounce twice before a player returns it, and the second bounce can be outside the court.

Argentine wheelchair tennis player Oscar Diaz during a match in Brazil, 2002

Rule
When serving, the wheelchair tennis player must keep the rear wheels of the chair behind the baseline until the ball is hit.

Glossary

advantage	the player who scores the first point after deuce is said to have the advantage, since winning the next point will also win the game
backhand	swinging the racquet back to hit the ball with the back of the hand facing forwards
ball boys and ball girls	young people who retrieve balls to keep the court clear during a match
baseline	the line that marks the back of the court
deuce	when players are tied at '40 all' and one player or pair must win two points to win the game
doubles	a match between two teams of two players each
fault	an error made while serving
foot fault	a fault caused by the server's foot entering the court before the racquet makes contact with the ball; a foot fault also occurs if any part of the server's foot is on the wrong side of the centre mark, or the server is walking or running while delivering the serve
forehand	swinging the racquet back to hit the ball with the palm facing forwards
grip	the part of the racquet that the player holds
let	a stroke that does not count and must be replayed; this most often happens when a served ball touches the net before entering the proper service court
lob	a ball hit high into the opponent's court
love	the tennis term for a zero score
receiver	the player who receives the ball from the server
server	the player who serves or puts the ball into play
set	a group of six games in a match
volley	to return the ball before it hits the ground